Why enfp and infj personalities make a good match.................
   Why enfp and infj work well together...............................3
   Enfp and infj personality types 5
   Similarities between enfp and infj personalities.................7
   Compatibility of the enfp and infj in relationships............11
   Compatibility of an infj man and an enfp woman 12
   Compatibility of an enfp man and an infj woman 13
What is an infj door slam?...19
   What is an infj personality type? 20
   What is an infj door slam?...22
Intp vs. Istp personality types: what are the differences? 31
   What does istp mean?..32
   What does intp mean? 32
   What are the main differences between intps and istps?...34
   Reasoning: concrete facts vs. Abstract concepts...............35
   Focus: focused on the present vs. The future 38
   Drive: intense focus vs. a laid-back approach 40
   Interests: seeking technical or creative outlets 43
   Outlook: pragmatists vs. Idealists 45

Why enfp and infj personalities make a good match

Dating isn't easy. You might think you've found the one, only to discover your personalities just don't quite match up.

Often finding the right person begins with understanding more about yourself. The myers briggs personality test was created to do just that.

If you've ended up here, you may know already that you are either **an enfp or an infj personality type**. So what does that mean exactly?

Enfp (the champion) represents extraverted, intuitive, feeling, and perceiving functions of personality. Enfp's are creative, outgoing, and highly perceptive. When looking for a partner, the dynamic enfp often needs someone who can play on the same emotional field.

infj *(the counselor), stands for introverted, intuitive, feeling, judging. He or she might be the perfect person to keep up with the vivacious energy of an enfp. Infj's are the quiet counterpart to the more excitable enfp.*

Why enfp and infj work well together

Opposites attract, or so they say. Perhaps a more accurate phrase would be, opposites attract, but their similarities glue them together. This is especially true with an enfp and infj in dating.

Enfp and infj compatibility can be magic, with each person adding their own special ingredients and perceptions into the relationship.

Both personalities are guided by their intuition and a strong sense of feeling. Enfps and infjs understand each other in many ways, but that doesn't mean they are exactly the same.

You may wonder how these two types can be so compatible when key aspects of both seem so fundamentally different from the other.

- *While one is more outgoing and the other is more reserved, both are incredibly deep feelers.*
- *Their emotions run deep; however, their feet aren't so planted. Both types of people can find themselves lost in the abstract, heads drifting high above the clouds.*

In short, they are both the perfect sort of weird for each other. While others may find it hard to ground them, they find their home base in each other and can often bring each other back down to earth.

When an enfp has found their infj match, they often find an instant connection, whether as friends or lovers. it may feel to them as if they knew each other in a past life.

Their connection feels intrinsic and inevitable, as they both process the world in similar ways, while their differences create a harmonious balance.

Enfp and infj personality types

Infj personality types are the rarest type of all of the 16 myers briggs types, making up a mere one percent of the population. They possess a gift of wisdom and insightfulness early in their lives.

Their dominant function is introverted intuition, meaning they are constantly absorbing the outer world and processing it internally. Infjs are curious creatures, always wanting to know more about the mysteries of life. **They are highly perceptive to human behavior and emotions, especially with their partners, and they can see far past the superficial masks we adopt.** Infjs are also quite intelligent and require a partner who can keep up. They may discover that they are more compatible with extroverted personalities with similar levels of intuition. (yes, you guessed it, like an enfp).

Enfps, like their introverted counterparts, have a strong sense of intuition. However, their talents lie in *seeing the bigger picture, in seeing the world for what it is and what it could be.*

They don't want to get lost in the details, but would rather discuss the big ideas. They have an enormous capacity for empathy and are often incredibly inclusive and welcoming.

While an infj may find lots of pleasure in staying in and staying still, enfps need exhilaration. Never let an enfp get bored or stuck in a rut, or they may find themselves struggling with restlessness.

Similarities between enfp and infj personalities

Both of these personalities could be found in the same corner of a party chatting away endlessly about life's big questions, their favorite new album, or their inner feelings. They are constantly absorbing and filing away new information about each other.

However, you may find that the infj slips out before midnight, with only a few quick goodbyes before heading to bed, *while the enfp is still partying the night away.*

As the infj tucks in for a good night's rest, he or she may be thinking about how much they had in common with the person in the corner, never knowing they have different personality types. That's because these types are not all too different.

Let's look into what draws together an enfp and infj in dating. Here are a few similarities between the two:

Free spirits

Neither of these two types of people can keep their feet on the ground for too long.

To them, the world is a playground of new discoveries, and they want nothing to get in the way of their lifelong quest for knowledge and adventure. They would rather not be tied down by the practicalities of life.

Both infjs and enfps thrive when they can test the limits of their imagination. As long as they are secure and comfortable in their sense of home, there are no limits to what these two can do together.

Data gatherers

Both of these personality types are like researchers who were never given an assignment. They constantly ask questions and love learning about the people who surround them.

They love to dig deep and find out what makes a person tick. In a relationship, they might find that they understand each other's depths quite quickly.

Religious or spiritual

Both appreciate a connection to something greater than themselves.

While neither is completely inclined towards organized religion, they may understand a deeper cosmic connection in the world.

Whether they become fascinated with astrology or theology, they become obsessed with uncovering the great truths.

Spontaneous

Spontaneity might not seem aligned with an infj personality, but these curious learners will jump at the chance to explore with the right person by their side. Once an infj feels safe, they might just be up for any new adventure!

Class clowns

Both infjs and enfps view the world with a keen sense of humor and can crack each other up for hours on end. Comedy relies on observation and these are two of the most observant in the bunch.

Givers

These two love to give and be there for someone in need of a helping hand or listening ear. Their generosity is boundless, but they have to be careful, as they can often sacrifice their own needs for the sake of others.

Compatibility of the enfp and infj in relationships

So how exactly does compatibility work? it seems to fall somewhere between pure magic and formulaic science. Sometimes, everything can be right on paper, but the spark isn't there.

Compatibility requires a connection between the mind and the soul but also a shared openness. Two people can enjoy similar interests but find they are unable to be authentic and vulnerable with each other.

Enfps and infjs work so well because of their curious natures and desires to give. Being a giving spirit goes beyond just helping someone — it also means giving more of yourself to your partner. **It means allowing them to prime their curiosity not just about the world but also with you. Both of these personalities relish the openness of their partners and the mutual desire to learn more about each other.** *However, this can look very different depending on the sex of the personality type. Infj men can be quite different from infj women, and the same goes for enfps.*

Women and men have been socialized differently and struggle with very different expectations from society and from their partners.

Compatibility of an infj man and an enfp woman

This relationship can be very fruitful. An infj man is often more sensitive and perceptive to the feelings of his partner.

He may be more attuned to his girlfriend or wife's needs and emotions, which is highly important in a relationship with an enfp woman.

It is important to her that her voice is heard, even if she hasn't spoken. These two often have a powerful unsaid ability to communicate due to their similarities.

Compatibility of an enfp man and an infj woman

It is important in this type of pairing that both voices are heard. An enfp man could easily fall into the trap of believing himself the smartest in the room. An infj woman will not let that slide easily, as she is his intellectual match.

However, when both partners give the other room to speak their minds, this can become a powerful duo. An infj woman can unearth deep love from an enfp man who may tend to stuff down his overwhelming emotions.

The two may get into a few heated debates when their natures get the best of them, but they are also highly capable of working out any issues through open communication.

Difficulties in enfp and infj relationships

With any relationship, there are going to be difficulties. a compatible match on paper doesn't always account for the tricky complications that life can throw your way.

However, don't let complications discourage you, as they are the spice of life — something that both enfps and infjs crave. Every difficulty comes with an opportunity to understand one another better, a new puzzle for these curious creatures to solve.

Here are a few potential problems to keep in mind as you move forward in your relationship:

- **Enfps can be overpowering.** These extroverted people can often get overly excited as their brain fires off new ideas at a million miles a minute. This can be frustrating for their more quiet and thoughtful partners who would rather have a conversation than a fired-up debate. Some enfps can speak over people, and this can really rub infjs the wrong way, even if they aren't the recipient.

- **Infjs can be perceived as controlling.** Infjs have it all figured out, or they think they do. Once they have a plan set in motion, they are hard-pressed to take advice. Enfps can find this frustrating, while an infj may find an enfps nature too indecisive.
- **Their mutual need for harmony can result in chaos.** Communication between enfp and infj partners can sometimes get tricky. When both partners desire balance, they may end up doing anything to prevent disruption and negative confrontation. This can lead to ineffective communication and arguments that camouflage deep-seated resentment. it's important

that both parties utilize their communication skills to be open and honest with each other, even if that means temporarily upsetting the balance.
- **Enfps could get bored.** An enfp may be searching for a new adventure while the infj just wants to stay put. The enfp longs to go to the party while the infj wants to start the new season of **westworld**. Learning how to compromise is crucial, and sometimes that means a solo adventure for the enfp.

Make the most of your enfp and infj relationship.

Are you an infj in a burgeoning relationship with an enfp or the other way around? This is an exciting time for you both, as a whole world of possibilities has opened up with a partner by your side.

Take the time to understand how your different personalities function, together *and apart. Understanding yourself will only help to elevate your relationship with your significant other.*

You both have the potential for a beautiful, loving partnership, full of laughter and new discoveries — since you have found your mirror in each other.
May your compatibility and deep souls nourish and inspire you both as you build a unique relationship together.

What is an infj door slam?

Maybe you know an infj and have witnessed the phenomenon known as the infj door slam.

Or maybe you're the door slamming infj who would like to better understand why you do what you do with people who've exhausted your compassion.

After all, cutting people off completely is not your go-to. it's a last resort. it's not something you enjoy doing to anyone, but when you reach that point, it becomes easy to walk away from the one who's crossed the line. You can do it without hesitation – and without feeling anything but relief.

It's not a zen thing. it's the infj's way to protect themselves from someone who has hurt them deeply — probably someone they thought or hoped they could trust.

But is it permanent?

And do all infj people do this?

Or more importantly, is there a way to open the door again?

And what would it take?

What is an infj personality type?

As the rarest myers briggs type personality (less than one percent of the population), the infj is known for being compassionate and quick to forgive those who've hurt them.

Unfortunately, this also makes them a target for those who take advantage of anyone who seems to value relationships and service to others over their own emotional well-being.

If you're an infj introvert, you know that just being around people is exhausting. But since you want to be there for those you care about — and you want to forgive those who've hurt you as soon as they show the slightest sign of remorse — you often put aside your need for alone time *to serve the needs of another.*

So, when someone crosses the line and shows zero signs of remorse for it, you're already feeling raw, exhausted, and vulnerable.

And when someone you want to trust kicks you when you're already down (either because of them or because of someone else), you feel it more.

What is an infj door slam?

Most of this book will be written as though you are the infj introvert. *If you're reading this as the friend of an infj, my hope is that this will help you see the door slam from the infj perspective.*

Once an infj has made up his or her mind to slam the door on someone, every avenue of connection is closed off.

- *Social media connections*
- *Phone access (by blocking numbers)*
- *Social avoidance*
- *Possibly even a change of locks (if necessary) or moving*

If you're an infj and you still have to be around the one you've shut out, you cut them off emotionally. You can still be civil, but even if the person who's hurt you is acting in a pleasant manner and reciprocates the polite small talk, you don't allow them any closer. Your guard is up, and you keep them at a comfortable distance.

They can access your remote self but not your essence, because around them, you're operating in "safe mode," like a traumatized computer.

You respond to them by numbing yourself — much as someone might become numb as a reaction to prolonged emotional abuse. You choose to feel nothing because every good feeling you used to have toward this person reminds you of their betrayal. And every negative feeling drags you down and makes you feel worse.

It's just easier to go into "machine mode," act as though everything's fine, and go on about your day while remaining completely inaccessible — emotionally — to the one who hurt you.

Why infj's cut people off from themselves

What's important to remember, here, is that you're not just protecting yourself from further judgment, criticism, or other hurt but also from the pain behind them.

You're protecting yourself as much (or more) from the internal sufferings of the one who hurt you as from any other hurt he or she might inflict if you let your guard down.

It's your empathy that keeps you raw and vulnerable, and sometimes shutting others out is the only way to give yourself the space you need to recover.

The ones who hurt you the most are often (if not always) the ones who are also in the most pain. And you feel that pain along with their attacks. And it's too much.

If you have every reason to expect more of the same from this person, it only makes sense to protect yourself by slamming the door shut between you. You might even go so far as to seem to shift personalities from infj to intp, favoring logic over emotion and avoiding any expressions of emotion that might tear open wounds that haven't yet healed.

After all, it's so much easier to focus on logic than to address emotions. Shutting yourself off emotionally and focusing on solving a puzzle probably energizes you, while being around people and empathizing with them drains your energy like nothing else can.

So, once you learn how to shut that door, why not keep the whole world at arm's length?

Because while you might have shut someone out of your life (or out of your inner circle), you remain sensitive to the needs of others. They draw energy from you. And while it's exhausting, you have a strong desire to help others heal and grow. You wouldn't have it any other way.

But if you're in an infj relationship, *and you're the one who slammed the door on* the other, you probably need time to process the pain and recover from it.

And if you're living with the person whom you've shut out, the best you can do when you have to be around them is to go numb and become emotionally unavailable.

Shutting people completely out of your life is not something you want to do. However long it took to get to this point, you still need time to honestly reflect on why you slammed the door and whether there's anything the other could do or say that would justify reopening it.

How to open the door when you've wounded an infj

If you're the one who's had a door slammed in your face, and you sincerely want to make amends and reconnect with your infj friend, keep the following in mind:

- *Give the infj person time and space. Don't try to rush them into reopening the door.*
- *Make gentle overtures to show your genuine remorse and to make amends, without expecting anything in return. As badly as they may want reconciliation, an infj can sense when there are strings attached.*
- *Be your authentic self — only more aware of the pain you've caused and more willing to do what it takes to rebuild trust.*
- *Don't assume you know how badly you've hurt them or how long it should take them to "get over it."*
- *Treat them as you would want to be treated, and don't do or say anything that you wouldn't take well if you were on the receiving end.*
- *Show them how important your relationship is to you — in*

ways that your infj friend will find meaningful. Hint: it should cost you something (not necessarily money).

Never say never.

While keeping all this in mind, brush up on your infj facts. it also can't hurt to find out what your own myers briggs personality type *is, if you don't already know.*

You might find you and your infj friend are more alike than you thought — or that your differences are what make your friendship so important to you.

In any case, don't lose hope. If you want true reconciliation badly enough, and if you're patient and willing to do what it takes to rebuild trust, that door will reopen when your infj friend is good and ready.

Don't cheat yourself out of that possibility by giving up too easily and thinking, "i've really blown it this time. He (or she) will never let me back in."

If your relationship is worth the time and effort to rebuild it, and you make the investment day in and day out, the infj you hurt – who also has a strong desire for reconciliation and harmony – will most likely notice.

Your relationship probably won't return to what it was before the door slam, but if you've succeeded in getting an infj to reopen the door – and if you persist in treating your friend as you want to be treated – there's every reason to hope your relationship will become even stronger.

So, may your thoughtfulness and compassion influence everything you do today.

Intp vs. Istp personality types: what are the differences?

People with **intp and istp personality types** tend to share many traits and behaviors.

Intps and istps are often logical, analytical, and focused.

These individuals have the drive to excel, but they go about their pursuits in different ways.

Istps are typically confident in their choices while intps may second-guess every decision.

This leads to different life paths for the average intp or istp.

Here is a closer look at some of the other **differences between these personalities.**

Quick note: studies show people earn more when they boost their self-

confidence. Confidence is a skill that you can improve.

What does istp mean?

The introverted, sensing, thinking, perceiving (istp) type is based on the myers-briggs four principal psychological functions.

These individuals are introverts who prefer internal reflection. They are logical thinkers but also open-minded.

Istps are sensing types, relying on specifics instead of abstracts to form conclusions.

They also tend to use logic over emotion when evaluating decisions.

However, they are also spontaneous and highly adaptable.

What does intp mean?

People with introverted, intuitive, thinking, perceiving personalities (intp) *are also introverts, logical thinkers, and flexible.*

They are perceiving types who enjoy keeping their options open instead of sticking to a structured approach.

As thinking types, intps rely on facts.

However, they are also intuitive, allowing them to use a combination of logic and abstract reasoning.

Instead of focusing on the present, they may look at the bigger picture.

What are the main differences between intps and istps?

Intp and istp personality types are based on the original myers-briggs type indicator (mbti).

The mbti relies on the four principal psychological functions proposed by psychiatrist carl jung.

Each person relies more on one of these functions most of the time, leading to different personalities.

Myers and briggs created four categories to express the dominance of these functions. These include:

- Introversion or extraversion
- sensing or intuition
- Thinking or feeling
- Judging or perception

Intps and istps share three out of four qualities from each category:

- Introversion

- Thinking

- perception

The main difference between intps and istps is related to their preference for sensing or intuition.

Your preference for sensing or intuition may impact the way you process new information. **Sensing people use their five senses while intuitive people are more abstract.**

Reasoning: concrete facts vs. Abstract concepts

Reasoning

Intps and istps may use different approaches for reasoning.

As istps rely more on their senses*, they prefer concrete details. They pay close attention to the raw data they hear, see, and touch.*

Sensing people are also more likely to use past experiences during the decision-making process.

Intps depend more on intuition and instinct for reasoning. They look for connections between abstract concepts and read between the lines.

Complex tasks

When tackling a complex task, **istps often break down the task into practical steps.**

They use a linear approach and complete things in sequence. Everything should have a beginning, middle, and end.

While performing the same task, **intps may focus more on the bigger picture and apply abstract models to find a suitable solution.**

Instead of breaking the task into practical steps, they may use a more fluid approach.

Flexibility

While intps and istps may have different preferences for processing information, both personality types remain flexible and open to new ideas.

Intps and istps are "perceiving" personalities. They are open and more exploratory in their reasoning.

Istps may carefully plan the steps needed to accomplish a task but can easily adapt the plan. They are not stubborn or rigid and openly accept new ideas.

Intps are also open-minded. Their abstract reasoning goes hand-in-hand with their inquisitive natures.

While both personalities are flexible and open, these feelings are often hidden from the outside world. Intps and istps are introverts and may not collaborate easily with others.

Focus: focused on the present vs. The future

Some people are dreamers while others are more grounded. **Intps belong to the first category. They tend to focus on the future instead of the present.**

Their intuitive nature compels them to explore possibilities without relying solely on available information.

Istps are more at home in the present as they focus their attention on what is real. They often ignore or minimize abstract qualities related to past experiences and future possibilities, preferring to use concrete factors.

Immediate vs. Future results

Istps may even become narrowly focused on their present tasks.

One of the characteristics of present-oriented istps is the need for immediate results.

Instead of completing activities to achieve a future goal, istps are more *likely to complete activities that bring an immediate reward.*

Intps are more future-oriented. They base decisions on anticipated consequences. For example, intps may use if/then reasoning to examine multiple outcomes.

They may also work backward from the anticipated results to come up with the correct course of action.

Instead of wanting instant gratification, intps are more comfortable completing tasks that contribute to long-term goals.
This also allows intps to become more goal-oriented and organized.

As goal-oriented individuals, intps are also less likely to engage in risky behavior.
Every decision is based on a review of potential outcomes. However, intps are "perceiving" people.

They are willing to change their plans and keep all options on the table.

Stress and anxiety

Remaining future-oriented may keep intps from fully enjoying the present.

The combination of introversion and intuition leads intps to internalize their worries and anxieties.

These individuals are more likely to suffer from social anxiety and other anxiety disorders.

Intps may also experience more stress from negative outcomes compared to istps.

They may not cope well with failure due to the amount of time spent analyzing future consequences.

Drive: intense focus vs. a laid-back approach

Intps and istps are often flexible and spontaneous. They are open to change and adapt to situations as they occur.

However, when it comes to planning or completing a task, istps often become intensely focused while intps remain laid-back.

Intps consider future outcomes. When it comes to achieving the desired outcome, they use unstructured processes.

Structure

Many people spend most of their time at work on unstructured processes.

These are the day-to-day tasks that allow businesses to run, such as attending meetings or receiving feedback.

Intps often thrive at these tasks and dislike heavily structured environments.

Along with preferring unstructured work, intps may perform better in creative learning environments. The rigid structure of a traditional classroom may cause intps to lose interest, resulting in lower grades.

In a work setting, structure may lead to decreased productivity or job performance.

Istps prefer structure and clear instructions. They work linearly to complete their goals.

As mentioned, istps are also present-oriented. Remaining centered and introverted may lead to greater attention spans.

The drawback to this personality trait *is a narrow-minded focus.*

While istps are open-minded, they may become too focused on the present to detect other possibilities.

Interests: seeking technical or creative outlets

Istps tend to prefer concrete facts and details compared to abstract concepts.

As a result, they tend to gravitate toward technical pursuits.

Istps are more likely to seek careers that rely on their technical aptitudes, *such as:*
*Architecture
Engineering
Programming
Financial planning
Medicine
Istps enjoy work that offers clear results. They dislike abstract tasks or open-ended projects. Everything should offer specific outcomes.*

Intps are more likely to thrive on creativity and ambiguity.
They enjoy work that allows them to consider theoretical possibilities. They become inspired by new ideas and may become easily bored by repetitive routines.

Examples of jobs where intps tend to excel include:

Graphic design
Photography
Fashion
Interior design

These are careers that give intps the freedom to focus on their internal talents and creativity to achieve subjective goals.

Both intps and istps tend to perform better when allowed to work on their own.

While they are often capable of working with others, they perform best without distractions from others.

Outlook: pragmatists vs. Idealists

Another interesting difference between intps and istps is their typical outlook on life.

Istps are often pragmatists while intps are frequently idealists.

The following characteristics help describe the pragmatic istp personality type:

Results-oriented
Willing to compromise to reach goals
Focused on the bottom line
Having realistic expectations

Istps follow practical steps to achieve results.

They also tend to act based on specific situations instead of abstract ideas.

For example, when confronted with a challenge, istps review the immediate implications of the challenge while intps focus more on the consequences.

Intps are often idealistic.

They frequently have lofty goals or ambitions. Unfortunately, without the structure and practical reasoning employed by istps, intps may struggle to reach their biggest goals.

For these reasons, intps may take longer to pursue their passions. Istps *typically discover their career paths early while intps are often late bloomers.*

Are you an intp or an istp?

Intps and istps possess many of the same personality characteristics.

They are introverts, thinkers, and perceivers instead of extroverts, feelers, or judgers.

The primary difference between these two personality types is their focus.

Intps are intuitive individuals while istps rely on their senses. This manifests itself in many ways including different outlooks on life and approaches to accomplishing goals.

Istps tend to use logical reasoning based on concrete facts. They are also present-oriented and prefer using practical steps. Intps thrive in unstructured environments and often have big ambitions.

There is also a spectrum for each of the characteristics discussed. Some intps may be more practical than others while some istps may have lofty dreams.

Where do you think you fall on the spectrum?

Made in the USA
Las Vegas, NV
30 January 2022